HOW TO ANALYZE PEOPLE

Reading Body Language Psychology (To Recognize Personality Patterns, Understand People And Gain Influence)

By

Joshua Strachan

1

Other Books by the Same Author

Thank you for purchasing this book. I believe that the change, improvement or the transformation you need will be manifested even as you read further. As you become equipped to be a winner in every aspect of life, below are other similar books you may find interesting and life-changing:

Persuasion Psychology: How to Influence People (Master the Art of Power and Mind Control Techniques)

Emotional Intelligence: How to Improve Your IQ, Achieve Self-Awareness and Control Your Emotions

Happiness Hack: The Beginner's Guide to Happiness

The Creative Treasures: 100 Creative Ways to Boost Your Creativity, Gain Recognition and Establish Authority

Memory Improvement Techniques: How to Develop a Brilliant Memory, Recall Things Faster and Achieve a Speedy Learning Ability

The S.M.A.R.T. Goals: How to Get Rich with No Money or Education

61 Ways to Attract Women According to 61 Experts: The Ultimate Seduction Guide to Become the Alpha Male Women Can't Resist, Unlock Her Legs and Make them Fall in Love

How to Become Successful in Life: Motivational Self Help for Wealth Creation and Life Strategies

Secrets to a Successful Long-Term Relationship: The Key to a Passionate Marriage and Sex Life

Table of Contents

INTRODUCTION

Even though body language can be picked naturally, and be responded effectively, the best social influencers actually take their time to go in-depth on the body language cues, primarily in order to react and to say things that will affect significant effect on people.

They are greater leaders and they influence people in ways you can't even imagine.

According to a scientific study, we only mean 7 percent of what we feel, 38 percent from the words we say and 58 percent from the body language.

Learning how to interpret above 50 percent of people's expressions will keep you ahead of social conformity, and you will always have the social leverage to make people do things and to make sure your goals are achievable, especially if it involves several people that you need to control.

You will have the ability to control and to influence people that have high emotional intelligence, because it all comes down to understanding expressions and actually knowing what somebody wants beyond their words.

Your main aim is to focus on the power of unspoken words, to empathize with allies and to make sure you react advantageously to the body language of a potential costumer, friend or a business partner.

RESISTANCE

Crossed Arms and Legs

Crossed arms and legs often show resistance to certain ideas or proposal.

It also shows criticism on the side of having different view, and when the person is not willing to listen to your ideas because he already made up his mind to disagree with you.

These physical posture often suggests that the other person is not trying to be open about what you are saying. If you observe closely you will realize that their response regardless how polite may not agree with the said opinion or proposal.

Also, do not get carried away by face expressions or the things that comes out of their mouth.

Body language tells more about people than any other form of expression. This is a natural form of resistance displayed by all men and most of us do it unconsciously to create a barrier between the opinion that is coming and the one we already have.

It is an attempt to block physical, emotional, and mental interference. Nobody does this intentionally except the people that have studied body language and have the aim to make you uncomfortable as they share a different value with you.

FACIAL EXPRESSIONS

Check The Eyes Crinkle

When people smile from the bottom of their heart, the muscles surrounding the eyes also respond to the smile.

The mouth can lie a hundred times but the eyes have never been a professional liar.

When someone smiles at you genuinely you can see the wrinkles at the sides of the eyes, often regarded as crow's feet. With the absence of the crow's feet be assured that something is being hidden and the smile is not coming out because you actually made them smile.

It might not be about you because the person may be hiding what they are thinking in order to avoid looking like they don't have the social ability to remain relevant.

On the other hand, the person may be hiding some emotions and trying as much as possible to look happy even as you are making the effort to put a smile on their faces.

Anytime you are cracking a joke or making statement that includes sarcasm, look at the corners of your listener's eyes to see if they are hiding something.

One way to realize the differences in different people is by actually waiting for an opportunity to see them laugh at something involuntarily—something or someone they are not obligated to impress.

MIRRORING CONCEPT

Body Language Mirroring Is a Good Thing

When you are in a meeting with someone and you notice that they fold their arms or wrist just after you do, or cross their legs every time you do the same, then that person is actually into the conversation and there is the highest tendency of him agreeing to almost hundred-percent of the things you are saying.

This is very important to recognize because that way you can put everything on the table since you know this person has less resistance.

Sometimes people lean their heads the same way you do when having a conversation, mirroring your body language, this means they already feel the bonding power coming over them. They are already feeling a bond but not consciously.

Receptiveness may not be read or analyzed just by the words someone says.

You don't need to ask people whether they are okay with an opinion or not before you increase the power of influence or the word power to get them on board.

Through their body language you can entirely analyze the situation and make sure that you do well in influencing them.

Negotiating will become easy and you don't have to go back and forth about the same thing. This will also help you in choosing the right party for achieving something great in the future.

THE STORY

The Story That the Posture Tells

Posture defines authority and the level of confidence someone has in an environment or about a particular subject matter.

You can recognize a leader through posture. These people have a respectful demeanor, and the confident posture may not be conscious because they have practiced long enough that it has now become a second nature.

Erect posture, expansive gestures, and the gestures often made with faced down palms signifies some amount of power and ownership. It also shows some amount of territoriality.

In case you want to experiment, enter an organization and start walking straight, with your shoulders placed back a bit.

Firstly, you will realize that you have occupied more space. People will effectively try as much as possible to create a space for you.

Secondly, people will begin to call you Sir or Mam, regardless how young you look.

In the case of leadership or the assumption of power, your dressing will ultimately affect your body language, thus the amount of time you will be able to hold on to the confident gestures and postures.

On the other hand, when having a conversation and you observe the person particularly "slouching," it means there is a depreciation in power because they are allowing more space.

Observe if this started happening when the conversation was initiated.

When people think you are more powerful and important in a conversation, they tend to give you more space, head down, and their tone will also be significantly affected by your presence.

Remember, these things are done unconsciously and fast.

Only good observers and the people that are willing to take social influence to the next level recognize and use this to their advantage.

All in all, maintaining a good posture will bring about respect, people would like to engage in a conversation with you even when they know clearly that you are not the leader.

THE EYE EXPRESSION

As stated earlier, the eye cannot follow the rest of the body in spreading lies into the world.

Remember in the movies when the star will ask a woman "look me in the eyes and say you don't love me?" or our parents when they say "look me in the eyes when talking to me?"

The theory has been around for quite long and it is still believed that a person should find it hard to hold a gaze when lying to someone. In the 21st century people have now become professional lairs and they can hold a gaze for as long as possible just to convince you that they are telling the truth. Eye contact is not a problem even when people are lying out of their minds.

In this case you will realize that people that hold eye contact longer than normal are the liars.

Reverse has been the case when someone is trying too much and putting too much effort into covering their lies. They will hold eye contact to the point they make you feel uncomfortable and even affecting their intonation.

An average person holds eye contact for 7 seconds at least and 10 seconds at most. And this only happens when you are listening and not talking.

If you are actively talking to someone you shouldn't be able to hold eye-contact for long. When a person does not blink and especially make you squirm when they stare at you, just be sure that something is amiss, and it is your job to find out by looking for other ways. For example, their face expression or their gestures could be telling you something else.

THE DISCOMFORT SIGNAL

Raised Eyebrows

Fear, worry, and surprise naturally make people's eyebrows to raise. This natural response of our eyebrows to such emotions are often unconscious, we unknowingly allow the eyebrows to stay hanging for a very long time especially when we are worried about something.

When having a casual conversation or when watching a comedy, try raising your eye brows, you will find the expression really hard.

When talking to someone and you observe a raised eyebrow, try and find out which of the emotions you are stimulating.

If you are not saying something that will actually cause surprise, then there must be fear or worry.

If fear and worry are out of the question, they definitely are surprised about something. In the moment, you can pause

and drift a bit to see where their interest
goes.

Remember, most people do these
unconsciously but you can take that as an
advantage to lead the conversation.

PLAIN ANXIETY

Anxiety About Approval: Exaggerated Nodding

This occurs mostly between bosses and employees, and also between students and teachers, but could occur even in personal relationship with people.

When someone nod excessively when receiving an instruction from you or when you are talking casually about something, be sure that this person needs your approval about something and they are working hard to get it.

Not only working hard, they are also worried about your decisions to either approve or disapprove them.

Also, they are worried about what you think of them, whether you are doubting their efforts, whether you think they are brilliant enough or whether you are doubting their ability to follow simple instructions.

All in all, you have all the right cards in your hands and you have the chance to ask them questions further in case you

are actually doubtful about something
that has to do with them.

STRESS

A Clinched Jaw

Also, in the normal world, people try as much as possible to hide stress and frustration. But something that has to do with both physical and mental balancing might be a bit hard to hide.

So, furrowed brow, tightened neck or a clenched jaw show the sign of discomfort mostly from stress.

The person might be saying something different just because they want to keep working or feel the need to impress you but these signs should provide you with the insight on the decisions to make that may favor this person or yourself.

Also when having a conversation with a stressed person, their mind could be anywhere, so observe if there's a considerable lack of concentration in addition to furrowed brow.

This might happen also when the conversation is deviating towards something they are really anxious about.

Given the situation and the type of conversation you are having, it is very easy to figure out whether someone is stressed or not.

You will often notice a significant amount of mismatch between what the person is saying and what their body is telling you.

Observing such mismatch may take long-term practice but exposing yourself to social interactions and meeting more people every day will speed up your learning.

ULTERIOR MOTIVE

Eye Contact Avoidance

When someone is trying as much as possible to avoid eye contact, be assured that this person is trying to hide something or they just did something wrong. Sometimes this happens when someone does not feel capable or deserving in the sense of relationship.

They will try as much as possible to look like they are just focused on what they are doing.

Over-focus is always suspicious, and deceit or lies can also be detected through that. This happens mostly in the office between coworkers or between kids and parents.

The aim for knowing peoples body language is to actually to know what is going on around you.

You don't need to understand everything about their body language. Just focus on the most important part—to learn what words cannot express. Focus solely on

language mismatch and you will be
surprised by the things you will find out.

OTHER BOOKS BY THE SAME AUTHOR

Persuasion Psychology: How to Influence People (Master the Art of Power and Mind Control Techniques)

Emotional Intelligence: How to Improve Your IQ, Achieve Self-Awareness and Control Your Emotions

Happiness Hack: The Beginner's Guide to Happiness

The Creative Treasures: 100 Creative Ways to Boost Your Creativity, Gain Recognition and Establish Authority

Memory Improvement Techniques: How to Develop a Brilliant Memory, Recall Things Faster and Achieve a Speedy Learning Ability

www.ingramcontent.com/pod-product-compliance
Lightning Source LLC
Chambersburg PA
CBHW051402250726
48656CB00006B/2232